Raising Ducks for Beginners Guide

Carson Wyatt

© 2017

Table of Contents

Introduction

Many people want to raise chickens when they think of food, but raising ducks is actually known to be easier. They are even great foragers amongst gardens, picking out slugs and other critters that can cause harm to your vegetable garden. There are many duck breeds that supply a large and nutritional supply of eggs, and they can be raised for their meat as well.

Reasons to Choose Ducks

You may still be wondering why you should raise ducks over chickens, but look at some of the reasons below. There are many reasons that people choose ducks over chickens, but it's a personal preference as well. This section will also help to make sure that you've thought about keeping ducks. With how long they live, this is not an easy commitment to make.

- **They're Healthier:** Ducks are healthier than chickens because they spend most of their time in the water. They aren't as susceptible to external parasites like mites, but chickens get infected by them often. Most parasites that try to latch on ducks will drown. Ducks also have a better immune system, which makes them less likely to contact disease.
- **Better in the Cold:** Ducks have another layer of fat that chickens don't have. They even have waterproofing on their feathers, which will help to protect your ducks against the elements. This means that they're more likely to do better in cold climates.
- **Heat Tolerance:** Ducks have a higher heat tolerance as well, meaning they do well in tropical weather too so long as they have a pond to swim around in.
- **They're Quiet:** Chickens aren't quiet, and so they can be a pain to raise. Of course, ducks are, which is another reason that

you might want to choose them. Male ducks don't cause the same ruckus as roosters do either.

- **Duck Eggs are Better:** Duck eggs are commonly considered superior to chicken eggs because they have a richer flavor and they're larger. They are known to have more nutrition in them as well, and they have a larger amount of protein. Duck eggs also are less likely to break and have a longer shelf life than chicken eggs. Many bakers swear by duck eggs for baking cakes and breads!
- **More Eggs:** Ducks actually lay eggs more regularly as well. You'll usually get three to four eggs from a female duck daily, and they lay year round as well.
- **Less Aggressive:** Ducks aren't as aggressive with their pecking order, so you can usually introduce more ducks later on without any serious problems.
- **Better for the Lawn:** Ducks are easier on your lawn as well

because they won't scratch it bare like chickens will. Ducks will trample it a little bit, but they won't mess with the basic greenery.

- **Pest Control:** Ducks are good for pest control as well, and they eat many critters that can be detrimental for your garden as stated before.

Now you know all the reasons you should choose ducks as part of your smart homesteading plan, All that's left to learn is to learn how to raise ducks so that you can get started.

Chapter 1: Raising Ducks FAQ

In this section, you'll learn a little bit about the most frequently asked questions and their answers before moving forward with your raising ducks guide. There's no need to worry about common questions.

What's a good drake to duck ratio?

Drakes being male ducks are actually needed for your flock. You don't want to keep too many drakes because it'll cause a lot of competition in you flock which will also result in over-mating. Ducks can actually be hurt by too much mating, and it can even lead to death if done in excess. You should only have one drake for every five ducks, which is good for light breeds. However, if you're only keeping two ducks, you can keep a single drake and a single duck.

Though, if you see she's losing too many feathers at the back of her neck or head, then your duck is being overbred. The back of the neck is where your drake will grab your duck during mating. If you do have too many drakes and you don't want to get rid of them by either slaughtering them for meat, selling or giving them away, then you can keep the drakes in a separate pin during breeding season from February to September.

Are ducks extremely noisy?

Not every duck breed is as noisy as the next. You'll find that there are some breeds that are actually quieter. If you're curious how noisy your ducks will be, then try to think about what breed you're going to get, what time of year it will be, and the number of ducks that you'll be getting. Call ducks, even though they're small, are the noisiest ducks that you can get. There are other miniature ducks that are fairly quiet, and when they do quack they can be quieter.

However, all ducks are a little noisy during mating season. Keeping your ducks housed before morning means that they'll be kept away from your neighbors even if they start to get a little noisy during the day. Most people don't consider ducks noisy with the exception of call ducks. If you're comparing them to chickens, then they aren't really noisy at all. Still, all animals will make some noise and you should keep this in mind. Don't forget to check to see if you are zoned to be allowed to keep ducks at all. If you aren't zoned, then you can get in a lot of trouble if your neighbors complain about the noise. You'll likely be fined and forced to get rid of your ducks.

Can chicken and ducks be raised together?

You'll find that different people have different opinions about if you can raise ducks and chickens together. Most people agree that they should be kept separate because you'll have a few problems if you don't. For one, you'll find that chickens and ducks will start fighting if you put them together. Chickens can cause damage to your ducks due to their sharp beaks as well. You'd also need to take extra precaution if you plan to keep cockerels (Juvenile Male Roosters) and drakes (Juvenile Male Ducks) together. Ducklings and chicks actually require different feed as well. If you don't keep separate waterers, then your ducks and can dirty your chicken's water as well.

Can you garden if you keep ducks?

This question is a little complicated. It really depends on what you're looking for in your gardening. If you're looking for a nice lawn and neat flowerbeds, then you can't usually do this unless you're going to completely fence off your garden from your ducks. If you want an orchard, then it'll be just fine. If you want a garden that produces vegetables then most ducks will be okay. They can help to keep critters out, but they're going to take some of your vegetables as well. It all really depends on the amount of ducks you have, what you're growing, and what types of ducks you'll be getting.

When can I expect eggs?

Ducks lay eggs around twenty to twenty-four weeks. They'll only start to lay eggs if you give them the correct food and lighting though. Otherwise, you can't expect eggs until it starts to warm up. You'll need to switch to a layer/breeder feed that has more vitamins and calcium for your female ducks when they start to lay. Your drakes will not want to eat this feed. Remember that the amount of eggs that you can expect will depend on the type of duck breed that you decide on.

Can you crossbreed ducks?

Yes, any duck that have can be crossbred with another duck. The only problem that can be caused would be the size. If you have a miniature, it will not always be able to crossbred with a normal sized duck. This can cause harm to your miniature, so keep that in mind when buying or raising your flock. However, there are times that your ducks can breed despite size differences. If you don't want your ducks to crossbreed, then you'll want to get one type of duck or keep them separate during the day and at night.

How do I tell my males from females?

With ducklings you won't be able to tell unless you know how to use vent sexing, but you'll find that you need to be careful if you don't want to hurt them. However, when your ducks are older, you'll find that males are usually slightly larger. You'll also find that drakes usually only make raspy noises. Female ducks are much noisier. During breeding season, you'll find that your drakes will grow colorful plumage for mating as well.

Do I have to clip my duck's wings?

This is completely up to you. However, if you don't clip the wings, then your ducks can actually fly away. Of course, if you have a pond it is much less likely that your ducks will fly away. If you have a small number of ducks, then spend a lot of time with them. Your ducks are less likely to fly away if they feel that they are attached to you. Ducks can often become attached to the people that are taking care of them, so this is a good preventive method.

However, make sure that you don't get too attached to the ducks if you plan to use them for meat. Remember that you should never name something that you're going to slaughter for food if you want to avoid emotional distress. Even if ducks do fly away, they may come back for occasional visits. Some people risk their ducks flying away by not clipping their wings so that predators won't get them. If your ducks can't fly, then you'll find that they are rather defenseless.

Do ducks always need a pen?

Even if you feel that you don't have predators around you, you'll still need to keep a pen for your ducks. There are many dangerous animals such as cats, raccoons, possums, foxes, weasels, hawks and even stray dogs that can be deadly to your ducks. This doesn't mean you need to lock your ducks up during the day, but you should keep an eye on them.

However, you will want to lock the in a pen at night for their own safety. Some people have to keep their ducks in a pen during the day as well. It all depends on the type of predators that you're dealing with, so you'll need to do your own research as well. Though, we'll talk more about predators in a later chapter.

Chapter 2: A Little about Duck Care

In general, you'll find that ducks aren't that demanding of an animal to raise. However, there are a few things that you need to keep in mind. Ducks are able to withstand many weather conditions and temperatures, and they're a great source of eggs, meat, and even feathers for pillows and more. Ducks can even make great pets, and they can outlive dogs because ducks can usually live twenty years or more.

About Ducklings

Take into account that duck eggs take twenty-eight days to hatch but this is after the parent has started to brood. For Muscovy ducks this takes thirty-five days. You have to make sure that your broody duck won't be disturbed so they don't' abandon their eggs prematurely. Once the duckling has hatched, make sure that they don't immerse themselves in water for at least a whole month. This will give your duck time for their preening gland to operate. The chick can catch a chill or drown beforehand since they aren't water proof until that gland becomes active.

Make sure that your nest is sawdust free if you're using shavings as well because sawdust can block the digestive system. This can lead to death if you aren't careful. There are many predators after your duckling as well, so make sure that they're well protected. You'll also need a heat lamp in case the mother does abandon them early. It doesn't happen frequently, but the heat should be gentle so that you don't overdo it and cook your ducklings. Luckily, you'll find that ducklings grow rapidly so after a few short weeks they can start to take care of themselves.

Dealing with Feeding Time

Ducks are good browsers, but they can't scratch at the dirt like chickens. Still, you'll find that they forage well. They will look around foliate, weeds, and even vegetable patches. Of course, that doesn't mean that they won't do a little bit of damage to your vegetable patch as well. They'll gladly eat slugs or insects that they find, and they'll even upturn stones looking for grubs. Some ducks will even catch small mice, and you'll need a pond or water of course as well. They'll eat small crustaceans as well as minnows if they find them. They can even eat young shoots of different water plants.

That doesn't mean you can get away from feeding them store bought food as well. This can be essential to giving them a healthy diet that will keep them producing. Still, with their foraging this means that you usually only need to feed your ducks once per day or twice per day depending on the species. The best way to give them enough food is to let them eat as much as they want but only for about fifteen minutes at a time. You can usually buy commercial pellets which is considered best because they're already balanced. Of course, you can also mash barley, oats, corn and more to help their diet. If a duck can't forage, you need to have a grit source ready for them. This will help them with egg production as well as their digestion. Ducks like variety in their diet as well.

Keeping a Water Supply

It's important to keep a water supply for your ducks as well. This can be a water course, a tub of water that they can drink from and bathe in or a pond. They need enough water to be able to immerse their heads in so that they can activate their preen valve that's under their tails, helping to clean their feathers. It's a part of their daily routine.

Ducks will even try to spill buckets of water near them, especially if they don't have a good source of water to clean themselves in and drink from. You'll need a waterer as well, and that's where nipple waterers or suspended waterers come in handy. Put them over a mesh area so that they don't get the bedding material wet either.it can be difficult to keep any area with ducks in it clean. Foul water can lead to eye problems and diseases.

Providing Shelter

Just like with any poultry, you'll need to provide shelter for your ducks as well. This will protect your duck from predators, critters and the elements. Ducklings are often killed by foxes, rats and more. You'll find that hooded crows and rooks will take ducklings as well. Of course, full grown ducks are often killed by predators as well if they aren't protected. There are different types of housing options that you can choose from depending on your situation. If you have a decent sized pond, then it offers protection during the day for your ducks from foxes and dogs. You'd just need a shelter for them at night.

Of course, most people don't have the luxury of having a large pond for their ducks. So you'll need a large shed and a closed area of open ground that they can forage on. Ducks won't roost like chickens, but they huddle together for warmth if the weather is cold. You'll need a shed that's about two to three square foot for each duck. You'll need to change bedding often because duck excreta contains about 90% water as well. You can use shavings, straw, corn cobs that have been ground and even newspaper for your bedding.

Just make sure that whatever you use it's dry and kept mold free. If a duckling is under seven days old, make sure that you aren't using dusty shading. If your bedding isn't checked regularly, you'll find that aspergillosis, which is caused by mold, can devastate your poultry. You'll need to have adequate ventilation for your ducks during warmer weather as well. Don't forget to provide a nesting box either. Of course, you need to watch out for ducks laying eggs wherever they stand as well. You'll need to provide a gently sloping ramp for them to enter and exit the shed as well. If they struggle, they can damage their webbed feet.

A Pen Perimeter

If you are having issues with stronger predators such as coyote or foxes, then you'll need to keep your ducks secure with an enclosure. This means that you'll need to construct something called a run, which is an enclosure that's built with stout timbers, and it's usually covered with two inch galvanized weld mesh or PVC covered weld mesh. You may be thinking it's a tad excessive, but predators like coyote for example can chew through regular chicken wire.

You'll need to sink your wire into a trench around the perimeter, sinking it to about twelve inches or so. Make sure to fold any slack towards the outside of your trench. It should then be covered by one inch galvanized chicken mesh, and then add backfill. This will keep out smaller critters such as stoats and weasels which will also kill your ducks and ducklings. You'll need to have two inch galvanized wire that covers the enclosure and keep your height about six feet. This will let you to walk into the enclosure and move through it easily. You'll learn a little more about predators and how to build a predator proof pen for your ducks in a later chapter.

Chapter3: A Little about Duck Health

Luckily there isn't too much worry about getting you duck sick, but there are still some things that you need to keep in mind. There will be times that you duck needs a little more care during ill health or due to an accident. Prevention of sickness is always better than a cure, and there are some simple steps that you can take to make sure that you keep your ducks happy and healthy. You should keep the environment they're in free from any sharp objects or obstacles as well as to keep it clean. Of course, there are things that your ducks are prone to.

Common Ailments

You'll find a list of common ailments as well as what you can do about them below. Most of these ailments will make you seek out a vet for your ducks, so it's best to have the contact information of a vet in your area that will treat ducks before you begin to raise them. This is one expense that you'll need to take in account with raising ducks even if you're just raising them in your backyard.

- **Aspergillosis:** This is labored and heavy breathing. It's extremely similar to pneumonia, and it can be caused by moldy bedding easily. It can also be caused by unclean bedding which will cause mold. You can treat it using fungicidal remedies, but managing your bedding is usually best. If you can keep it mold free, then it's going to prevent it in the long term.
- **Coccidiosis:** You'll find that there are a few symptoms to look out for but you usually start to notice blood in their droppings first. You'll then see thin, weak birds. This is because their gut lining is being attacked from the inside out. This happens in hot wet conditions usually because the

ground starts to become infested by Coccidia. You'll need to go to a vet to get this treated. You can avoid problems in the future if you make sure that young ducklings graze on green grass, and make sure to move their grazing area on a regular basis so that it doesn't become infected or polluted.

- **Mites:** You'll notice your first symptoms of mites by the excessive scratching because they cause irritation through blood sucking. Infected birds coming into contact with other birds is what causes the infection, but it can also be where other infected birds were grazing. You can treat mites with pesticides, but make sure to be careful with the instructions, especially the withdrawal time for treatment.
- **Botulism:** You'll find that symptoms include loss of control in wing movement, legs and even necks. It can also cause your ducks to have an inability to swallow. This

happens when you let your ducks graze near rotting vegetables or animal waste or near it. It's a result of bacterial infection, and prevention is always best. You need to prevent them from swimming in polluted water as well. Make sure you always give your ducks clean water for drinking, and seek advice from a vet if you feel this is afflicting your ducks.

- **Maggots:** You'll usually be able to see maggots, but dirty and dry vent is a system as well. This can be due to giving your ducks too little water, meaning they won't be able to drink or bathe enough. You'd need to pick the maggots away from the area, and then treat with a suitable ointment or spray. You'd get that from your vet, and you'll need to make sure that they have enough water in the future. Internal problems can result of a severe infection, and if that's the case the duck would need put down.

- **Respiratory Issues:** When your ducks are sitting hunched up or they're bobbing their heads with their tail up, then they're having breathing issues. It's often caused from a bacterial infection, and it can happen in extremely wet weather. You'll need antibiotics from your vet.
- **Sinus Problems:** You'll often notice puffed up cheeks and weeping nostrils. This is caused by bacteria as well, which means you'll be seeking antibiotics from your vet. This can lead to hardened cheeks that are incurable if left untreated. You usually need antibiotic injections to cure this bacteria at all.
- **Worms:** This can first be seen by noticing a drop in the eggs that your ducks produces. It can also cause your ducks to have an increased appetite, which can be caused from tape worms or round worms. Ducks can pick these up from foraging on dirt, infected ground. Worm

tablets can usually be obtained from the vet.

- **Lameness:** You'll notice limping in your ducks, and it can be caused by quite a few things. Make sure that there are no sharp stones or sharp fragments in the area. Your duck's webbing on their feet can easily be infected or split, and their legs can be damaged through careless handling as well. Take care of the wound if that's the cause of lameness, and isolate them on a bed of clean straw until they heal.

Chapter4: Building Predator Proof Housing

You already know a little bit about providing housing for your ducks, but this chapter will go a little more in depth to make sure that you can keep your ducks completely safe. It is not an 'if' your ducks will be eaten because if you do nothing it is a 'when' your ducks will get eaten. This chapter will also go over common mistakes so that you don't endanger your new ducks.

Rule for Building a Pen

There are some rules that you need to keep in mind when you're trying to build a pen. If you keep these rules in mind, then you'll be able to build a pen that is much more secure.

- **Rule 1:** Build your pen in order to keep predators out. Don't build it in mind to keep your birds in or you'll make many common mistakes. It is easy to contain birds, but it is harder to keep coyotes, foxes, raccoons and other predators out. You should do some research to find out what predators are in your area, and build your pen in order to keep those specific predators out.

- **Rule 2:** Remember that everyone has predators around their ducks. Just because you live in a city doesn't mean that there aren't predators in your area. You may not see raccoons and possums, but they are there as well. You'll even find that coyotes are being found in many urban areas as well.
- **Rule 3:** Your ducks will get eaten if you don't do something. As I said in the beginning of this chapter, you can't ever assume that it is an 'if' your ducks get eaten.
- **Rule 4:** Bad pens are actually worse for your ducks than having no pen at all. If your pen isn't secure, it will actually trap your ducks in even though the predator is in there as well. This

will make them an easy meal for the predator that gets in.

- **Rule 5:** You can't just protect them from predators as they come. You need to take preventive measures because if not you'll lose many ducks along the way. It is you're responsibly to keep your ducks safe once you decide to raise them.

Common Mistakes:

Below you'll find a few common mistakes to avoid and a little bit about how to avoid them. There are many common mistakes that you might make because many people underestimate how smart a predator can be.

- **Roofing:** You need to make sure that your pen has a roof. So many people seem to think that a tarp counts, but it just won't work. Your roof should be made of a heavy wire if you don't make a solid roof entirely.

Raccoons are very destructive, and they are very smart like most predators. Predators will often chew through a tarp in a short amount of time. Tarps can also accumulate water which will cause them to collapse. Tarps just aren't a long term or safe solution for the roof of your pen.

- **Chain Link:** You shouldn't assume that chain link fences are predator proof. Many raccoons can eat your duck even through a chain link fence. Raccoons will actually scare ducks to one side and another will pull the ducks head through the fence. You need about four feet of hardware cloth around the bottom of your cage. Of course, you can use any solid material such as wood. Make sure to put hardware cloth along the inside if that is what you decide to use.
- **Flooring:** You actually need a floor on your pen as well because predators can both climb and dig. You cage needs

to be fully enclosed for your ducks. However, that doesn't mean that you need a solid floor. You can actually use wire. The wire can even be buried under the ground. Keep in mind that raccoons can actually lift chain link dog kennels though, so you need to make sure that it's secure.

- **Door Latches:** You need door latches as well because raccoons can open doors and lift latches. It is best to use a padlock or a carabiner clip to help secure your door latches.

Knowing Your Predators

If you want to protect your ducks against predators, then you should know your predators. That's exactly what this section is all about. If you know what to protect against, then it should be easier to protect against them. For example, if you don't have bobcats, mountain lions or bears in your area, then you'll be able to protect your ducks without as much cost or effort.

- **Weasels:** This is an easy predator to have around you, and they can get into even small holes. They will kill birds even if they don't plan to eat all of them. They just plan to come back for the dead birds later, so it's important to buy hardware cloth.
- **Raccoons:** This is an extremely common predator, and they're agile as well as smart. They can loosen boards and put them back too. They will even test things for weaknesses to see if they can get in.
- **Bobcats:** Bobcats, mountain lions and bears are in the same class of predators, and they are both strong and vicious. They will need a solid construction to protect against. You can't keep these predators out with hardware cloth or chicken wire.
- **Opossums:** It is a debate on if these predators actually eat birds that aren't already dead.

Still, it's best to protect against them.

- **Foxes:** These are tough to protect against because they're both fast and smart. They can even climb and dig.
- **Pets:** Cats and dogs can attack your ducks as well. Even if a dog is just trying to play with your duck, they can kill them by injuring them while playing. They can also carry pasteurella which is toxic to most birds.
- **Raptors:** This is mostly a problem during the day, which is why you need a top to your pen. Horned owls, which are seen at night, can often kill smaller ducks. Other large predator birds are something you need to watch out for as well.

Chapter 5: From the Yard to the Table

This section might not interest you if you're only keeping your ducks for their eggs and as pets, but ducks are a great source of meat. This section will cover how to use ducks for meat, so you'll need to learn how to humanely slaughter them and dress them. There are some things you'll need to keep in mind, such as not naming your ducks, especially if there are kids around. It can cause emotional distress if you name a duck and then eat it. A homesteading shouldn't have more than one or two pets because slaughter is a part of the natural cycling for raising an animal for meat. It is completely different to prepare something for yourself to eat and prepare something of commercial sale, and the advice in this chapter is only meant for your personal use.

For Eggs

When you're keeping your ducks for egg production, they may still end up on your table. Of course, there's a difference when you're keeping them for mostly eggs versus meat. Ducks start to produce eggs at about four to five months old, and they lay for much longer than chickens. A good laying duck can lay for five to six years, but as it gets older there will be a gradual decrease in the number of eggs it lays. If you keep the ducks without a male duck, often called a drake, it's said to cause a better egg yield.

Slaughtering Your Duck

There is debate about what is the best way to slaughter your duck. The time you should slaughter your duck will also depend on type of duck you're raising. Larger ducks, including the Rouen breed, are often big enough to slaughter at eight to twelve weeks. However, with a smaller species such as the Khaki Campbell, you'll want to wait until about sixteen to twenty weeks. Of course, there's a basic rule to keep in mind as well. Younger ducks have more tender meat.

Take into consideration the amount of food you're feeding them as well. Is waiting for them to become larger worth the amount you're spending on the feed? Pin feathers can be harder to remove from older birds as well. Before you slaughter your duck, you should have your duck fast for about twelve hours with only water to drink. This will give it time for the crop to empty, and it'll reduce the risk of contamination when you're dressing your duck. You need to kill your duck as humanely as possible because there's no reason for a duck to needlessly suffer.

There are a few different methods that can be used to kill a duck humanely. You can tie the bird's wings together with twine and then place it in a bag, leaving the head out. Canvas bags are usually best, and the neck should be protruding completely. This will keep the wings from flapping wildly which would make it harder for you to get a clean cut and kill it quickly. Then you will want to grip the bird firmly by its legs, laying the neck under a broom handle laid firmly on the floor.

Put your feet on either side of it, and tug upwardly sharply. At the same time you'll need to stamp down hard on the broom handle to break the neck. You need to make sure it's placed firmly on the ground otherwise you'll just crush the neck and not break it properly. This will cause unnecessary suffering. If you pull too hard the head can come off entirely which is messy but it's still a clean death. Cut the head off or slit the throat afterwards, and then hang the bird upside down to bleed it.

Plucking is Next!

You can use hot wax to remove feathers by submersing your duck in a bath of hot water and melted wax, and then removing the down feathers once it's cooled and your bird is coated. Of course, there are two traditional ways to pluck as well, and those are wet and dry plucking. For dry plucking, you simply pull the feathers from the bird while it's warm. You'll need to pull wing and tail feathers sharply out straight, and you'd need to hold your bird firmly. Make sure to pull the feathers against the grain, but you have to be cautious not to tear the duck in the process. This will have a clean carcass, and it's easier to pull the down feathers.

Wet plucking is much easier, and you have to heat up a barrel of water around 140 degrees F (60 degrees C), and then dunk the bird in it by holding onto its feet. This will make your feathers easier to remove, and it's less likely to tear the bird up. Of course, this can cause some discoloration to the flesh of the bird, especially if you accidentally hold it under too long. Your job doesn't end when the feathers are removed though.

You can use the feathers as down for a pillow stuffing or a duvet. You'd just need to separate the down, which is small and fluffy feathers from the large feathers found on the winds and tail. Small body feathers can be used for duvets and pillows. You want to wash both with a gentle detergent, then scatter them on a surface that is made of a porous material. Make sure they're completely dry before using them. You can place them in a tumble dryer as well.

Eviscerating Your Bird

This is the messy part about raising your ducks for meat. You need to start by inserting a sharp knife into the vent at the rear of your duck, and slit the flesh up all the way to the breastbone. Insert your hand high into the body cavity, and pull out the internal organs. You then need to remove the head, and cut off the legs at the hock joints as well. Wash your duck inside and out, making sure to be thorough. If you want to keep the billets, wash them thoroughly as well, placing them in a suitable plastic bag. Place that bag in the carcass or keep them separate. You should dress a bird as soon as possible, and then they can be stored in a fridge for five to seven days.

Chapter 6: Some Duck Breeds

You know the basics of raising your ducks now, but you still need to pick a duck breed to work with. What breed you pick is completely up to you and there are pros and cons with each breed. This chapter is all about showing you the basic information on different duck breeds so that you can make your own educated decision on which one to purchase and raise.

Khaki Campbell

This duck is a cross between Rouen, Runner ducks and Mallard ducks. It originated from England around the

19th century. They weigh about three to five pounds, and it's one of the largest breeds out there. It's a great egg layer, and they can lay around 320 eggs each and every year. They are not a good brooder, and they will not usually hatch their eggs at all.

American Pekin Duck

These were originally bred from the Mallard duck that's from China. It's also known as the Long Island Duck, and it's a favorite for domestic duck breeds. This duck accounts for 95% of the meat that's consumed in the US. The Crested Pekin lays a fair amount of eggs, which is over 200 a year. You should not allow it to incubate them or it will drop or stop. If you want to hatch the eggs, use a broody hen because these ducks are known for abandoning the nest far before the eggs are even hatched. They are an intelligent species, making them good pets as well. This makes them a favorite among kids.

Indian Runner Ducks

This is a largely popular duck that has an upright posture and a very long neck. It give sit an almost mischievous look, and these ducks come in a variety of colors. They like water, but they're happy foraging amongst vegetation and leaf litter the most. They can be used to train dogs and sheep, and they run rather than waddle. These ducks can lay a little over 250 eggs each yea, and they just drop them wherever, so you'll have to keep an eye out. Be careful or predators will steal these eggs right out from under you.

Rouen Duck

It's hard to tell the difference between a Rouen hen and a Rouen drake, and they almost have the same appearance as a Mallard. The Rouen are just slightly larger, and the colors are a little bolder as well. This is mostly bred for a meat duck, and it usually weighs about nine to twelve pounds. The egg production is significantly lower at 30-120 eggs a year though.

Muscovy

This duck has a distinct taste in meat since it isn't descended from the Mallard. It is great for people that like their meat dark and with a strong flavor. It also has less fat so it's much leaner, and many people compare it to roast beef or even veal. The males can grow up to 15lbs, and females are generally about half the size.
However, they can be crossbred with Mallards frequently, resulting in a "Mullard" which is considered "kosher". If you have neighbors near you, then this duck is a popular choice

because they are extremely quiet. They also come in different colors, but black and white or just white ones are most common.

Bantam Duck Breeds

These duck breeds are also known as miniature ducks, and they can be called "call ducks" as well. This duck was originally bred in order to lure ducks to the guns for hunting. They're about ¼ or 1/3 the size of their larger counterparts. These are not usually raised for the meat, but they do lay a decent amount of eggs. They can also make good pets for kids as well. These ducks can be fly away a lot, so you sometimes need to clip their wings. They can also attract buzzards, kites, foxes and other predators due to their size. They are good sitters, and they are good at keeping garden pests under control as well.

East Indies Bantam

This is a miniature breed that is favored by those that want to exhibit birds. They have a striking black color that has a sheen to it, and they are quieter than most call ducks. They make good flyers as well, so you'll need to clip their wings. Keep them in a closed environment such as a cage or run if you don't want to clip their wings.

Silver Appleyard Miniature

This is another popular bantam breed, and it's incredibly friendly. They are very sociable, so they chatter a lot. They even show their excitement by chattering, but they don't lay many eggs. They make good sitters though, and they are quite healthy.

Traditional Call Ducks

We mentioned call ducks earlier, and they are considered to be a miniature duck that will call others with their loud quacking. Many hunters use them, hoping to lure larger duck breeds. They are good at foraging, and they are a hit with kids as well.

Keep in Mind

These ducks may not be what you should raise for meat or eggs, but they can be used for both meat and eggs as well as sitters. You can also use them as a great decoration for your home. Remember that you can have more than one duck breed, but you may have issues with them getting along if you aren't careful. Still, most miniature ducks do get along with older ones, especially traditional call ducks. Remember not to get a call duck if you have neighbors or it can cause many disturbances.

Chapter 7: More about Feeding Your Ducks

It can be daunting trying to figure out what to feed your ducks, especially if you don't want to stick to pellets. You already know that ducks forage so no matter what you feed them, just make sure that you don't overfeed them. Also, make sure that you give them a little variety as well if you want to keep them happy. Happy ducks are less aggressive and they're more likely to produce a large number of eggs. This chapter will go a little more in depth on what your ducks can and can't eat.

What They Can Eat

Below you'll find a few things that you can feed your duck to break up the routine.

- **Bird Feed:** Bird seed will make ducks happy because they actually love seeds. You can actually feed your ducks chicken feed as well. Just pick whatever is most cost effective, and they can actually eat scratch grains or any grains that chickens can eat too. Ducks even like layered feed, and if you have a female you'll want to give her a little more protein. This is needed for laying a good amount of eggs.

- **Cracked Corn:** You can give your ducks whole kernel corn, but many people believe that it's easier for your ducks to digest if you crack the corn first. However, other people believe that oils on the outside of your whole kernels can be better for your ducks.

- **Bugs:** Your ducks can forage, so they can find bugs on their own. Though, you can buy or raise bugs for your ducks as well. Ducks aren't picky about the bugs they eat, and they'll eat meal worms, night crawlers or almost any kind of insect.

Treats for Your Ducks

Sometimes you'll want to give your ducks a treat to keep them happy. These are needed in their diets, but you ducks will always appreciate them. Just make sure not to give your duck too much of any of the following. Moderation is key!

- **Fruit:** This needs to just be a treat for your ducks because it's unhealthy if they eat it in excess. Ducks love berries, seeded fruit, pit fruits, and melons. They can even eat watermelon rind, so there's no need to throw them away anymore. They can even eat fruit that's a little too ripe for you to eat, and they'll still love it.

- **Vegetables:** Ducks love vegetables such as peas, squash, cucumbers, zucchini, kale, or even broccoli so you can easily feed your duck these vegetables. Just make sure that they don't have pesticides on them if you're buying them from the store. Just make sure not to overpay for it.
- **Whole Grains:** Ducks love grains, but you shouldn't feed them anything but whole grains or they'll pack on too much fat. Ducks actually gain weight easily, so make sure to limit their whole grains. They enjoy snacks like whole wheat bread, brown rice, oats and quinoa.
- **Protein Foods:** Sometimes you need to add a little more protein in you duck's diet, so you can give them snacks with protein in them as well.

Scrambled eggs are actually a great way to feed your ducks proteins, but it can feel a little odd. This is great to feed them if you have too many eggs, which can happen during warmer months.

Some Food Supplements

Ducks are considered to be extremely simple animals even though they like variety. Of course, as long as they are healthy they will lay eggs. Food supplements are a choice, but they can help to keep your ducks happy and healthy.

- **Grit:** If your ducks have access to dirt, then they'll likely not need grit. Ducks will usually find small pebbles to eat to help to grind up their food. However, if they're in solid grass, you'll need to purchase a bag of grit to help them. Throw a handful or two in there are about once a week. This will help them to digest their food like they need to.

- **Oyster Shell:** If you are having an issue with your duck's eggs coming out pitted or with thin sells, then you might want to consider this supplement. This will give them the needed calcium to strengthen the shells of their eggs. You can usually find this at a local feed store as well.

What Not to Feed Your Ducks

Here are a few things that you need to avoid giving your ducks because it will harm their health.

- **Spinach:** Spinach can keep your ducks from absorbing calcium which will resort in eggs with thin shells.
- **Citrus Fruit:** This fruit will also keep your duck from absorbing any calcium, which will make your eggs easy to break.
- **Iceberg Lettuce:** This is able to be fed to you ducks in small

amounts, but with too much your ducks will usually suffer from diarrhea. This can throw your duck's whole body off.

- **Eggplant & White Potatoes & Green Tomatoes:** These are part of the nightshade family, and every part of their plants are toxic to ducks.
- **Raw & Dried Beans:** You can give your ducks beans if they are cooked or sprouted. Dried or raw beans are toxic to ducks.

Get a Feeder & Waterer

Get a poultry feeder and waterer to help you feed your ducks a little easier. If you don't want to worry about bringing food out once or twice a day, then you'll want to fill up a few poultry feeders for your ducks. Just refill them when you need to, and it will be harder for your ducks to waste food with this type of feeder. Of course, a poultry waterer is also a great way to give your ducks the water they need. Ducks will swim in any water they can, so they'll often get their drinking water dirty which can lead to health problems. It is harder for your ducks to dirty their drinking water if you have poultry waterers for them.

Chapter 8: 7 Bonus Duck Recipes

If you're raising ducks, then you're likely in need of duck recipes as well. Of course, you'll find that there are many delicious duck recipes that should be able to convince you to start right away.

Duck Breasts with Blackberry Sauce

Blackberry sauce pairs well with the rich dark meat flavor of duck breasts, and it makes a savory sweet dish in this recipe.

Prep Time: 15 Minutes

Cooking Time: 30 Minutes

Serves: 4

Ingredients:

- 1 ½ Tablespoons Butter, Unsalted
- 1 Tablespoon Honey, Raw
- ½ Cup Fruity Red Wine
- ¾ Cup Chicken Stock
- 1 Shallot, Minced
- ¼ Cup Blackberry Jam, Seedless
- 1 Tablespoon Fresh Thyme, Minced
- 4 Boneless Duck Breasts

Directions:

1. Start by heating your oven to 375, and rinse your duck breasts. Don't forget to pat them dry, and then season them with salt and pepper.
2. Take a nonstick pan, and put your duck breasts in with the skin side down. Cook until browned, and pour off any excess fat. Don't throw the fat away, and put your duck breasts on a roasting pan. Roast in the oven for about fifteen minutes, and now you can start to prepare the sauce.

3. Melt your butter in a small pan, and stir in your honey. Make sure to cook and stir until it's blended.
4. Stir in your wine, shallot, and stock, bringing it to a boil.
5. Add in your jam, and season with salt, pepper and thyme. Reduce the heat, letting it simmer for fifteen minutes. Stir occasionally and adjust seasoning to taste.
6. Bring it back to a low boil, and continue cooking until it thickens and is ready to serve.
7. Remove your duck breasts from the oven when they're done, and let them stand for a few minutes. Remove your fatty skins, and then serve them on a plate with your duck sauce on top.

Traditional Roast Duck with Citrus Sauce

The duck in this recipe is traditional and lightly seasoned, letting you taste the flavor of the meat. Duck is often served with sauce to compensate for the basic way it's cooked, and the citrus sauce in this recipe compliments it well.

Prep Time: 20 Minutes

Cooking Time: 2 Hours 45 Minutes

Serves: 4-6

Ingredients:

- 5 ½ lb Pekin Duck (or Long Island), Neck Reserved
- 1 Lemon, ½ Cut in Wedges with ½ Juiced
- 1 Navel Orange, ½ Cut in Wedges with ½ Juiced
- 2 Cups Water
- ½ Teaspoon Soy Sauce
- 2 Tablespoons Coriander Seeds
- ½ Tablespoons Butter, Unsalted & Softened
- 1 Tablespoon All Purpose Flour

Directions:

1. Start by heating your oven to 325, and prick your duck all over. Use a sharp knife, and season the cavity with salt and

pepper before stuffing it with your lemon and orange wedges.

2. Take a medium roasting pan, and combine your duck neck with your coriander seeds. Place the duck on the rack, seasoning it with salt and pepper. You can then set it in your roasting pan, covering it with foil. Bring the water to a boil over high heat, transferring it to the oven and roasting for an hour. Most of the fat should be rendered.

3. You can then transfer the duck to your work surface, and turn your oven to 350 now. Strain your pan juices into a medium bowl, skimming the fat off. Return the duck to the pan, and prick it all over once more. Roast again for an hour, but this time it needs to be uncovered.

4. Increase the oven to 400, tipping the juices from the cavity into your roasting pan and transferring your duck to a baking sheet. Make sure that baking sheet has a large rim, and roast for 45 more minutes.

The meat should be tender
while the skin is also crisp.

5. Set your roasting pan over high
   heat, and add your orange and
   lemon juices. Make sure to
   bring it to a boil, and add your
   reserved juices from the pan.
   Add in your soy sauce, boiling
   for another minute. Pour the
   liquid into a small saucepan,
   bringing it to a simmer over
   medium high heat next.

6. Take a medium bowl, making a
   paste with your flour and
   butter, whisking in ¼ cup of the
   liquid until smooth. Scrape the
   mixture into your saucepan,
   simmering over low heat again.
   Keep whisking until your sauce
   has thickened which will take
   about two minutes. Season it
   with salt and pepper again.

7. Transfer your duck to a carving
   board and let rest for at least
   ten minutes before carving.
   Serve it with your citrus sauce.

Crockpot Chinese Roasted Duck

You may have noticed that the recipes so far have been a little long, but not every recipe has to be complicated just because it has duck in it. This recipe is able to be cooked in your crockpot, making it perfect for anyone who's too busy.

Prep Time: 10 Minutes

Cooking Time: 4 Hours

Serves: 5

Ingredients:

- 1 ½ Teaspoons White Sugar
- 1 Teaspoon Sea Salt
- ¼ Teaspoon Black Pepper
- 1-3 Cloves Garlic, Minced
- 3 Tablespoons Ginger, Minced
- 1 Tablespoon Honey, Raw
- 2 Tablespoons Soy Sauce
- 5 Green Onions, Whole
- 5 lb Duck

Directions:

1. Start by putting a rack in your slow cooker, and then place your green onions on the rack.
2. Take a bowl, mixing your garlic, sugar, ginger, honey, soy sauce, salt and pepper together. Brush your duck down with this.
3. Put your duck in your slow cooker with the breast side up, and cook on high for four hours.
4. Serve while still warm.

Savory Duck Gumbo

This gumbo is made for two ducks, but if you want to serve less people then just cut the recipe in half. You'll find that it is easy to make, but the recipe is time consuming. Gumbo of any kind is served traditionally with rice, and wild rice goes great with this recipe.

Prep Time: 10-15 Minutes

Cooking Time: 1 Hour 5 Minutes

Serves: 8-10

Ingredients:

- 2 Wild Ducks, Chopped
- ½ Cup Canola Oil
- 1 lb Smoked Sausage, Sliced
- 2 Cups Onion, Chopped
- 2/3 Cup All Purpose Flour
- 1 ½ Cups Green Pepper, Chopped
- 1 ½ Celery, Sliced
- 2 Tablespoons Parsley, Fresh & Minced
- 14.5 Ounces Stewed Tomatoes, Canned
- 1 Tablespoon Garlic, Minced
- 2 Bay Leaves
- 2 Tablespoons Worcestershire Sauce
- 1 Teaspoon Thyme, Dried
- 2 Quarts Water
- 1 Teaspoon Thyme, Dried
- 1 ½ Teaspoons Black Pepper
- 1 Teaspoon Sea Salt

Directions:

1. Brown your duck in batches in oil, and then remove it to set aside. Discard everything but 2/3 cup of drippings. Add in your flour, cooking and stirring

over medium high heat until browned. This will take ten to twelve minutes.

2. Add in your onion, green pepper, sausage, celery, garlic and parsley. Cook for another ten minutes, making sure to stir occasionally.

3. Stir in your remaining ingredients, and add your duck back in. make sure to bring it to a boil, and reduce the heat. Cover and let it simmer for an hour to an hour and fifteen minutes. The duck should be tender.

4. Remove your duck, and debone it, cutting it into chunks. Simmer for five to ten minutes until heated through, and serve with rice.

Simple Crockpot Duck

Once again this recipe makes it easy to cook your duck up, and you don't even have to cook any sides. Everything is cooked in your crockpot, but many people do prefer to serve it with wild rice as well.

Prep Time: 15 Minutes

Cooking Time: 5 Hours

Serves: 4

Ingredients:

- 1 Whole Duck
- 1 Package Onion Soup Mix
- 4 Cups Potatoes, Peeled & Chopped
- 2 Cups Carrots, Chopped
- 1 Medium Onion, Chopped
- 2 Tablespoons Butter
- ½ Cup Water
- Sea Salt & Pepper to Taste

Directions:

1. Take your duck and remove the neck and giblets. Rinse under water, and wipe the duck dry. Make sure to dry the inside as well.
2. Place all of your ingredients besides your duck in the slow cooker, and then stir. Make sure it's all well covered by the water, and put the duck on top

of your vegetables. Cover it, and cook on high for about five hours. Serve with wild rice.

Maple Glazed Duck

This is a sweet duck recipe that doesn't take too long to make. The maple pairs well with the strong flavor of duck, and yet the glaze doesn't take long to make at all.

Prep Time: 15 Minutes

Cooking Time: 40 Minutes

Serves: 4

Ingredients:

- 4 Duck Breasts, Skin On
- ½ Teaspoon Cayenne Pepper
- 1 Tablespoon Brown Sugar
- ½ Teaspoon Sea Salt
- ¼ Teaspoon Black Pepper
- ¼ Cup Maple Syrup

Directions:

1. Take a sharp knife and trim off the extra skin from your duck

breasts. You shouldn't have overhanging skin. Slice a few slits into the skin as well, but try not to cut the meat.

2. Seas with salt and pepper with the skin down, putting them on a skillet over medium high heat. Cook your breasts for about five minutes, but try to use a cold pan to start with. This will help the fat to render from the skin. Your skin should start to brown after five minutes, and then flip them so they can brown on the other side as well. Cook for about two minutes before flipping again.

3. Cook in your oven for four minutes at 400 with the side with skin down.

4. Mix all other ingredients together in a bowl, and then put your maple glaze on your duck breasts. Have the skin side up, and return them to the oven for another four minutes. Let rest before slicing.

Simple Orange Duck

This orange duck is best paired with gravy, which is why it's in your ingredients list. You'll find that orange duck doesn't have to be hard to prepare, but you do need to baste it quite often.

Prep Time: 15 Minutes

Cooking Time: 2 Hours

Serves: 4-6

Ingredients:

- 1 Duck, Washed & Dried
- ½ Teaspoon Garlic Powder
- ½ Teaspoon Onion Powder
- 2 Tablespoons Brown Sugar, Packed
- ¾ Cup Orange Juice Concentrate
- 1 Orange, Sliced
- 2 Tablespoons Orange Marmalade
- ½ Teaspoon Sea Salt
- ¼ Cup Flour
- 1 Package Brown Gravy Mix

Directions:

1. Start by preheating your oven to 350, and then grease a 9x13 pan.
2. Place your orange slices in the cavity of your duck, placing in a prepared pan.
3. Combine all of your sauce ingredients and then pour them over your duck.
4. Bake for two hours, but make sure to baste every fifteen minutes with your orange mixture.
5. Cook your gravy, and serve with your duck.

Conclusion

Now you know everything that you need to know to raise ducks in your own backyard. There's no reason that homesteading needs to be difficult, so now you're able to raise ducks easily with this guide. Just start by picking the duck breeds that you want, and use the knowledge that you found in this book to get started. All you have to do is determine the size of your flock after you pick out what ducks will work best for you. It should be easy to take care of them now that you know everything you need to.

Also, one more thing. If you enjoyed this book, please leave a review on Amazon. It will be greatly appreciated.

Thank you very much and good luck to you,

Carson Wyatt

http://www.FunHappyLives.com